FABRIZIO SILEI • MAURIZIO A.C.QUARELLO

Rosa's Bus

darf
children's
books

Grandpa had been promising Ben for such a long time to take him to Detroit. He said he wanted to show him something.

'But what are we going to see, Grandpa?' Ben asked a thousand times on the journey.

'Wait and see,' replied the old man. 'Don't be impatient.'

Spelling out the words, Ben read:

'HEN-RY FO-RD MU-SE-UM'.

Ford's Museum! Wow, Grandpa's really lost the plot, he thought.
We've come hours and hours by bus to see some old cars.

*Is Grandpa mad about cars? Who knows? He doesn't even have a
licence...*

But, hang on, it's not a car museum! America's history is inside.
It's the Henry Ford Museum of Innovation, home of American
history.

'There's one thing we've come to see,' Grandpa said, 'and we're
not stopping here to talk about it. Just follow me and that's that!

'First though, I have to go to the bathroom. My prostate went to
sleep while we were on that bus.'

*Grandpa always has to go because of this prostate, Ben thought. Who
knows what it is or where it came from, but he's always complaining
about it.*

He came out of the men's room looking calm and happy as if
he'd seen paradise.

A big, tall man in uniform directed them
down a long corridor,
through a garden
and into a room with an old bus.

'There it is,' he says pointing to it, 'It's that one over there.'

'Hurry up or you'll miss it!' he added jokingly.

'**That's the one!**' grandpa exclaimed.

'**Good heavens, that's really it!**'

For a moment, Ben was afraid the bus was really going to leave. He looked around to see if, by any chance, there might be something else to look at. In one corner there was a big portrait of a woman with a medal on her chest.

Disappointed and confused, Ben looked at Grandpa.

Ugh! An old bus.

Grandpa smiled, showing his remaining teeth.
Poor me, thought Ben, *he's really gone off his rocker.*
It must be the prostate.

'Sit there, right there, in that seat. It's Rosa's seat!'

Before Ben could ask him who this Rosa was, Grandpa started telling a story.

In 1955, I was 26, and lived in Montgomery, Alabama. I hadn't studied much, but I knew how to read and write.

There weren't classes with children of every colour then, like yours. Black people had their own schools, their own bars, their own public baths, their own lives.

White people tolerated us because they needed the work, but they wanted nothing to do with us.

On the door of many bars, a sign was hung that read

WHITES ONLY

forbidding black people to enter.

'Like today, for dogs?' Ben asked incredulously.

Worse. Today, if a dog goes into a bar by mistake, it's sent outside. Back then, if a black person had tried that, he would have been lynched on the spot and the killers would have been found innocent.

I was a porter at the station. It was hard work. Some white people were nice and would even leave a tip.

But most of them treated us with contempt, as though we were slaves.

I was young, and it all made me feel so angry.

To keep the anger down though, I'd think of the fear... and about Jeremy.

Or, better still, Jeremy's eye and leg.

Tall and powerful as an oak tree, Jeremy was a porter too.

He was fifty years old, with a glass eye and one leg stiff as a broom handle. Everyone knew what had happened to him.

One day, when he was still a boy, a suitcase he was carrying on Platform Seven fell down. It fell open, and the immaculate clothes were scattered about the rails, dirty with dust and coal.

Amongst the shirts and waistcoat there was a white hood with two holes for eyes.

The next moment, the owner of the suitcase began hitting him with his silver-headed cane.

He hit him with all his might, but Jeremy seized hold of the cane and disarmed him. He didn't touch the man, didn't even brush him. But, bending it over his knee, he broke the cane in two and threw it onto the tracks along with the clothes.

He was sacked on the spot.

Then night fell.

A group wearing the white hoods with eye holes beat him bloody with iron bars and canes until, sure that they'd killed him, they drove away.

But he got through it, and when he recovered, he was taken on again at the station. His glass eye and his rigid leg were a warning to us all.

It was the most terrible story Ben had ever heard.

He still could not understand, however, why his grandpa had to tell it to him right there on the old bus in the museum.

It was 1st December 1955, and as I did every night, I took the bus home - exactly the same one in which you're sitting now. The seats in front were reserved for whites. We could sit in the other ones, as long as there were no white people standing.

That evening it was cold and I was tired. Luckily, when I got on there were still some seats free and I could sit down.

After a few stops Rosa got on as well.

Rosa was forty two, wore glasses, and carried herself with dignity.

She was a woman of colour, like so many others returning from work in the big women's store where she was a tailoress.

She sat next to me. Other black people were standing, but all the whites were seated. At the next stop four people with skin white as flour got on. The driver immediately yelled out for all the seats to be given to the whites. I obeyed, and so did two other black women. One seat was still needed, but Rosa did not move.

The driver realised and from his driver's seat yelled out again:

'All the blacks must get up and give up their seats up. You, get up and give the man a seat!'

It was at that point that something incredible happened, an extraordinary thing that was to change everything, making the days to come different from all of those before:

Rosa stayed unmoving and seated in her place.

The driver drew up to the kerb and stopped the bus. Swearing, he left his driver's seat and went over to Rosa. 'What's going on? Are you deaf? Can't you see that a gentleman's standing?'

Worried, I looked and Rosa and said: 'Madam, you must get up, otherwise you'll end up in trouble.'

She looked straight at me and saw my fear. I didn't say another word and neither did she.

That slender determined woman looked at me and made me feel less than nothing.

Now Grandpa's eyes grew sad and shiny. He took hold of Ben's hand and, squeezing it hard, continued.

Not a word. Only that look, full of pity. With his uniform on, a well-shaven neck and sweaty armpits, the driver looked completely helpless before her.

'Get up!'

'**No,**' she said tranquilly. Calm and serence she looked the driver straight in the eye.

'I've told you to get up and give up your seat to the gentleman!'

Rosa didn't move a muscle. She just repeated 'No!'

The man stormed off the bus gesticulating and shouting: 'So it's like that! Now. I'll make you see. I'll sort out this nonsense!'

Despite the fact that it was December, it began getting hot on the bus, unbearably hot. Some of the whites shook their heads.

'Where are we going to end up?' said a lady, looking at us resentfully.

An old black man standing near me went up to Rosa.

'Lady! There's still time. Get up!' he said to her, almost begging. She looked at him calmly, smiled and shook her head.

Then the driver returned with two policemen who took hold of her by force and lifted her up off her seat.

She stayed motionless and let them carry her to the car like a queen on a throne. They handcuffed her like a criminal. I did nothing,

NOTHING AT ALL.

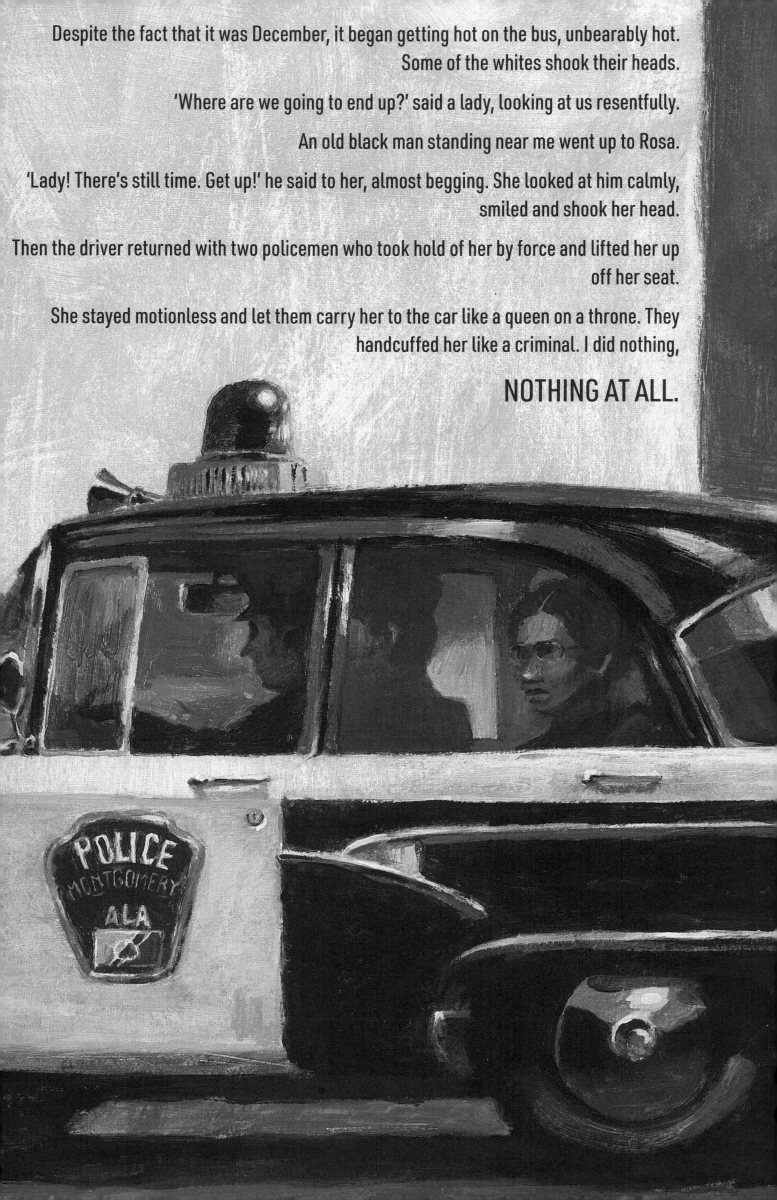

I stayed standing there, frightened, and thought the woman must be mad, that she'd pay dearly for stepping out of line.

At home, I didn't tell them anything, but the whole night I still saw that woman's eyes, and I couldn't close my own.

A few days later, at work, they told me that when I went home I shouldn't take the bus.

Jeremy told me, looking at me with his good eye. 'Why not? Do you know how far my house is?'

'They've arrested one of our women, on a bus, because she didn't want to give up her seat. So, we're protesting, and not taking the bus. Understood?'

I was ashamed.

I didn't have the heart to tell him that I was on that bus too.

I only said I agreed and that evening I went home on foot.

It took me two hours.

Later on, I learned that they'd released Rosa almost immediately thanks to a lawyer and the help of a young pastor, but she had to pay a fine of ten dollars.

That pastor was Martin Luther King Jr and he blessed the boycott.

Everyone made the arrangements they could, travelling on foot, by bicycle, with a cart, by delivery van, even on horseback. Just not by bus. This went on for a whole year. The transport company was at risk of bankruptcy, and many drivers lost their jobs.

Rosa lost out too and because of threats to her life she had to move elsewhere.

But she did not give in and, in 1956, a year after her **NO**, the Supreme Court declared racial discrimination on transport unconstitutional.

Where you're sitting is the place Rosa occupied that day. The seat I'm in now was where I was sittting all those years ago. This was the place I gave up because I didn't know how to say **No**.

Look at the photos and see how much we owe her. There is no photo of your grandpa, because he was afraid - afraid for her too. On that day, history passed by me. It was a bus and it brushed against me and I didn't know how to get on it. Worst of all, I saw Rosa getting on and I tried to persuade her not to.

We thought she was mad, but it was we who were mad, so used to hanging our heads and always saying 'yes'.

That's why I've brought you here today, to remind you that there's always a bus which goes by in everyone's life.

I missed mine so many years ago. You keep your eyes open: don't miss yours.

'So…' stammered the old man, 'I wanted to ask your pardon.'

'Pardon for what, Grandpa?'

'For not having Rosa's courage, for not being on her level.'

Ben got up and hugged his grandpa. He squeezed him and looked at Rosa's photo. His throat tightened. *She was really just human. Her muscles were of no use, nor was force.*

All she needed was her big eyes and calm smile.

That's all I need to overcome fear.

While he was thinking all this, Grandpa freed himself from the hug, blew his nose and pulled himself together.

'Would you like an ice cream?'

'Yes!' replied Ben.

They went into a cafe, and felt as though they had time travelled. Ben and his grandpa ordered ice cream and ate it at the nicest table.

The old man picked up a newspaper, and on the front page was the photo of a young black man. His eyes were just like Rosa's.

FABRIZIO SILEI

Fabrizio Silei was born in Florence in 1960. He is the author of many books, essays, novels and short stories for children and young adults. He founded The Platypus Atelier, a community education project. In 2018, his novel The University of Tuttomio was a finalist for the Strega Girls and Boys Award. In 2014 he received the Andersen "Writer of the Year" award.

MAURIZIO A. C. QUARELLO

Maurizio Quarello is an award-winning illustrator and designer. In recent years he has picked up the Premio Andersen Award for best Italian illustrator. He also received the Llibreter award in Spain and the Libbylit award in Belgium. In 2013 he received the following awards: Prix Littéraire des Ecoliers, XI Prix Je lis J'elis, XV Premio Nazionale un Libro per l'Ambiente and Prix 2013 du Mouvement pour les Villages d'Enfants, in 2014 with the IBBY Silverstar in Sweden, Premio Orbil and Premio Fondazione Cassa di Cento in Italy, in 2015 with the Premio Laura Orvieto, 1st prize in Italy.

SIÂN WILLIAMS

Siân Williams has translated works by Dacia Maraini, Lalla Romano, Antonio Tabucchi and Francesco D'Adamo. She founded The Children's Bookshow in 2003, which takes writers and illustrators of children's literature from the UK and abroad on tour to theatres throughout the country every autumn.

Published by Darf Children's Books, 2022
An Imprint of Darf Publishers
277 West End Lane
West Hampstead
London
NW6 1QS

First published by Orecchio Acerbo Editore in 2011
Written by Fabrizio Silei
Illustrated by Maurizio A. C. Quarello
Translated by Siân Williams

A catalogue record of this book is available from the British Library.

Printed and bound by Elma Basim, Turkey

ISBN - 9781850773405

www.darfpublishers.co.uk